TREKKING THE TOUR DU MONT BLANC

IGN MAPS AND ESSENTIAL RESOURCES TO PLAN YOUR HIKE

JUNIPER HOUSE, MURLEY MOSS,
OXENHOLME ROAD, KENDAL, CUMBRIA LA9 7RL
www.cicerone.co.uk

CONTENTS

© Cicerone Press 2024
First edition
ISBN: 978 1 78631 229 7

MIX
Paper from responsible sources
FSC® C010256

Printed in China on responsibly sourced paper on behalf of Latitude Press Ltd
All photographs are by the authors unless otherwise stated

FFRandonnée
www.ffrandonnee.fr

The routes of the GR®, PR® and GRP® paths in this guide are reproduced with the permission of the Fédération Française de la Randonnée, holder of the exclusive rights of the routes. © FFR 2024 for all GR®, PR® and GRP® paths appearing in this work. Mapping © IGN 2024. Copying and reproduction prohibited.

lovelljohns.com

Where IGN mapping is not available for Italy and Switzerland, custom 1:25,000 mapping by Lovell Johns has been used. Contains OpenStreetMap.org data © OpenStreetMap contributors, CC-BY-SA. NASA relief data courtesy of ESRI.

The large cairn at the Col de la Seigne, looking into Italy (Stage 3)

TREKKING THE TOUR DU MONT BLANC

The Tour du Mont Blanc is one of the world's classic treks, a 170km long-distance walk through the magnificent mountain scenery of the Mont Blanc massif in France, Switzerland and Italy.

This map booklet of IGN 1:25,000 maps contains:
*   the full and up-to-date trail, showing the main stages, alternative stages and variant routes (shortcuts, high-level extensions and bad weather options)
*   town maps for Les Houches, Les Contamines-Montjoie, Courmayeur, Champex Lac and Chamonix
*   resources for planning your TMB: Route summary tables, Stage facilities planner, Overview profiles/staging options and Accommodation listings.

GPX tracks for the routes in this map booklet are available to download free at www.cicerone.co.uk/1229/GPX. A GPS device is an excellent aid to navigation, but you should also carry a map and compass and know how to use them. GPX files are provided in good faith, but neither the author nor the publisher accepts responsibility for their accuracy.

The complete two-way guidebook *Trekking the Tour du Mont Blanc* is available separately from Cicerone. It describes the classic anti-clockwise route in 11 stages starting from Les Houches near Chamonix; the reverse, clockwise circuit; plus variant options and alternative stages in both directions.

ROUTE SUMMARY TABLES

TMB anti-clockwise route							
Stage	Start	Finish	Time	Distance (km)	Ascent (m)	Descent (m)	Page
1	Les Houches	Les Contamines	6hr	17.5	1000	850	16
1A	Les Houches	Les Contamines	7hr 45min	19.0	1450	1300	16
2	Les Contamines	Les Chapieux	7hr 30min	19.0	1350	960	19
3	Les Chapieux	Rifugio Elisabetta	5hr	14.5	1100	460	24
4	Rifugio Elisabetta	Courmayeur	5hr 30min	16.5	530	1500	28
5	Courmayeur	Rifugio Bonatti	4hr 30min	12.0	1090	290	32
6	Rifugio Bonatti	La Fouly	6hr 30min	20.5	970	1380	37
7	La Fouly	Champex	4hr 30min	15.0	530	670	41
8	Champex	Trient	5hr 30min	16.0	890	1080	45
8A	Champex	Trient	7hr	15.5	1230	1420	45
9	Trient	Tré-le-Champ	5hr 30min	14.0	1150	1010	48
10	Tré-le-Champ	Refuge de la Flégère	3hr 30min	7.0	800	340	53
11	Refuge de la Flégère	Les Houches	7hr	18.0	890	1760	55
Totals main route			**61hr**	**170.0**	**10,300**	**10,300**	

TMB clockwise route							
Stage	Start	Finish	Time	Distance (km)	Ascent (m)	Descent (m)	Page
11	Les Houches	Refuge de la Flégère	8hr 15min	18.0	1760	890	58
10	Refuge de la Flégère	Tré-le-Champ	3hr 15min	7.0	340	800	55
9	Tré-le-Champ	Trient	5hr 30min	14.0	1010	1150	53
8	Trient	Champex	5hr 30min	16.0	1080	890	48
8A	Trient	Champex	7hr	15.5	1420	1230	48
7	Champex	La Fouly	4hr 30min	15.0	670	530	45
6	La Fouly	Rifugio Bonatti	7hr 15min	20.5	1380	970	41
5	Rifugio Bonatti	Courmayeur	3hr 45min	12.0	290	1090	35
4	Courmayeur	Rifugio Elisabetta	6hr 15min	16.5	1500	530	32
3	Rifugio Elisabetta	Les Chapieux	4hr 15min	14.5	460	1100	28
2	Les Chapieux	Les Contamines	6hr 45min	19.0	960	1350	24
1	Les Contamines	Les Houches	5hr 45min	17.5	850	1000	19
1A	Les Contamines	Les Houches	7hr 15min	19.0	1300	1450	19
Totals main route			61hr	170.0	10,300	10,300	

Overview profile/staging options – anti-clockwise TMB

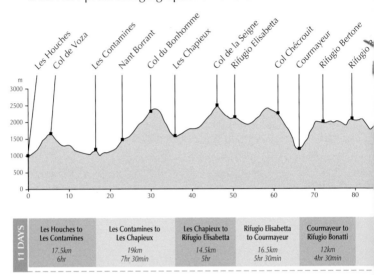

11 DAYS				
Les Houches to Les Contamines	Les Contamines to Les Chapieux	Les Chapieux to Rifugio Elisabetta	Rifugio Elisabetta to Courmayeur	Courmayeur to Rifugio Bonatti
17.5km *6hr*	*19km* *7hr 30min*	*14.5km* *5hr*	*16.5km* *5hr 30min*	*12km* *4hr 30min*

9 DAYS				
Les Houches to Les Contamines	Les Contamines to Les Chapieux	Les Chapieux to Rifugio Elisabetta	Rifugio Elisabetta to Courmayeur	Courmayeur to Rifugio Elena
17.5km *6hr*	*19km* *7hr 30min*	*14.5km* *5hr*	*16.5km* *5hr 30min*	*19.9km* *7hr*

7 DAYS		
Les Houches to Nant Borrant	Nant Borrant to Rifugio Elisabetta	Rifugio Elisabetta to Rifugio Bertone
23km *7hr 45min*	*28km* *10hr 45min*	*20.8km* *7hr 30min*

5 DAYS	
Les Houches to Les Chapieux	Les Chapieux to Rifugio Bertone
36.5km *13hr 30min*	*35.3km* *12hr 30min*

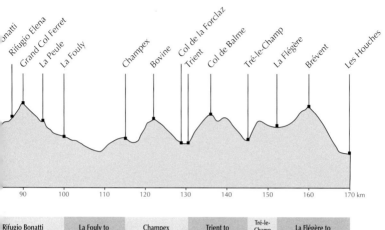

Rifugio Bonatti to La Fouly	La Fouly to Champex	Champex to Trient	Trient to Tré-le-Champ	Tré-le-Champ to La Flégère	La Flégère to Les Houches
20.5km 6hr 30min	15km 4hr 30min	16km 5hr 30min	14km 5hr 30min	7km 3hr 30min	18km 7hr

AVERAGE DAY – 15.4km / 5hr 30min

Rifugio Elena to Champex	Champex to Trient	Trient to La Flégère	La Flégère to Les Houches
27.6km 8hr 30min	16km 5hr 30min	21km 9hr	18km 7hr

AVERAGE DAY – 18.8km / 6hr 45min

Rifugio Bertone to La Fouly	La Fouly to Col de la Forclaz	Col de la Forclaz to La Flégère	La Flégère to Les Houches
28.2km 9hr	28.9km 9hr 20min	23.1km 9hr 40min	18km 7hr

AVERAGE DAY – 24.2km / 8hr 40min

Rifugio Bertone to Champex	Champex to Tré-le-Champ	Tré-le-Champ to Les Houches
43.2km 13hr 30min	30km 11hr	25km 10hr 30min

AVERAGE DAY – 34km / 12hr 10min

Overview profile/staging options – clockwise TMB

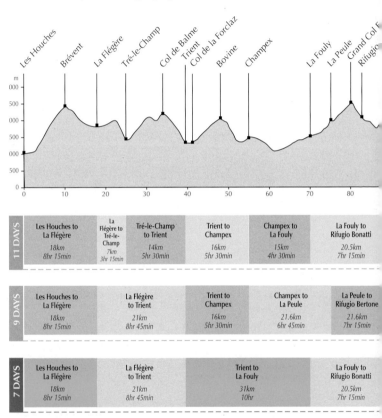

11 DAYS	Les Houches to La Flégère	La Flégère to Tré-le-Champ	Tré-le-Champ to Trient	Trient to Champex	Champex to La Fouly	La Fouly to Rifugio Bonatti
	18km 8hr 15min	7km 3hr 15min	14km 5hr 30min	16km 5hr 30min	15km 4hr 30min	20.5km 7hr 15min

9 DAYS	Les Houches to La Flégère	La Flégère to Trient	Trient to Champex	Champex to La Peule	La Peule to Rifugio Bertone
	18km 8hr 15min	21km 8hr 45min	16km 5hr 30min	21.6km 6hr 45min	21.6km 7hr 15min

7 DAYS	Les Houches to La Flégère	La Flégère to Trient	Trient to La Fouly	La Fouly to Rifugio Bonatti
	18km 8hr 15min	21km 8hr 45min	31km 10hr	20.5km 7hr 15min

5 DAYS	Les Houches to Tré-le-Champ	Tré-le-Champ to Champex	Champex to Rifugio Bonatti
	25km 11hr 30min	30km 11hr	35.5km 11hr 45min

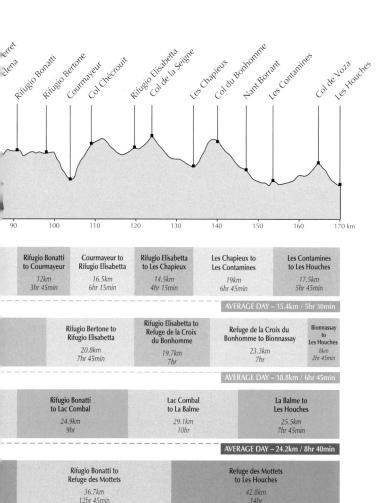

Rifugio Bonatti to Courmayeur	Courmayeur to Rifugio Elisabetta	Rifugio Elisabetta to Les Chapieux	Les Chapieux to Les Contamines	Les Contamines to Les Houches
12km *3hr 45min*	*16.5km* *6hr 15min*	*14.5km* *4hr 15min*	*19km* *6hr 45min*	*17.5km* *5hr 45min*

AVERAGE DAY – 15.4km / 5hr 30min

Rifugio Bertone to Rifugio Elisabetta	Rifugio Elisabetta to Refuge de la Croix du Bonhomme	Refuge de la Croix du Bonhomme to Bionnassay	Bionnassay to Les Houches
20.8km *7hr 45min*	*19.7km* *7hr*	*23.3km* *7hr*	*8km* *2hr 45min*

AVERAGE DAY – 18.8km / 6hr 45min

Rifugio Bonatti to Lac Combal	Lac Combal to La Balme	La Balme to Les Houches
24.9km *9hr*	*29.1km* *10hr*	*25.5km* *7hr 45min*

AVERAGE DAY – 24.2km / 8hr 40min

Rifugio Bonatti to Refuge des Mottets	Refuge des Mottets to Les Houches
36.7km *12hr 45min*	*42.8km* *14hr*

AVERAGE DAY – 34km / 12hr 10min

STAGE FACILITIES PLANNER

Stage	Place	Altitude (m)	Walking time	Cum. stage time	Distance (km)
1	**Les Houches**	**1007**	-	-	-
1	Col de Voza	1657	2hr 30min	2hr 30min	6.0
1	*Hotel Le Prarion*	*1860*	*+30min*		
1	Fioux	1520	15min	2hr 45min	0.8
1	Bionnassay	1326	20min	3hr 5min	1.2
1	**Les Contamines**	**1161**	**2hr 55min**	**6hr**	**9.5**
2	Le Pontet	1180	40min	40min	1.0
2	Notre-Dame de la Gorge	1210	20min	1hr	2.8
2	Nant Borrant	1459	45min	1hr 45min	1.7
2	*Refuge des Prés*	*1935*	*+1hr 30min*		
2	La Balme	1706	1hr	2hr 45min	2.5
2	Refuge de la Croix du Bonhomme	2433	3hr	5hr 45min	5.8
2	**Les Chapieux**	**1554**	**1hr 45min**	**7hr 30min**	**5.2**
3	Ville des Glaciers	1789	1hr 35min	1hr 35min	5.0
3	Refuge des Mottets	1868	25min	2hr	1.3
3	**Elisabetta**	**2195**	**3hr**	**5hr**	**8.2**
4	Lac Combal	1968	50min	50min	3.6
4	*Val Veny*	*see Stage 4 Facilities panel for details*			
4	Col Chécrouit	1956	2hr 40min	3hr 30min	7.3
4	Dolonne	1210	1hr 40min	5hr 10min	4.5

Legend: ▲ mountain hut　○ hotel　◒ camping　✳ bivouac　🍴 refreshments　⊕ shop　💳 ATM　ℹ information　◉ train station　◉ bus service　🚡 cable car

Cum. stage distance (km)	Ascent (m)	Descent (m)	mountain hut	hotel	camping	bivouac	refreshments	shop	ATM	information	train station	bus service	cable car
-	-	-	▲	○	◒		🍴	⊕	💳	ℹ	◉	◉	🚡
6.0	660	20					🍴				◉		
				○		✳							
6.8	-	130	▲			✳							
8.0	-	190	▲										
17.5	340	510	▲	○			🍴	⊕	💳	ℹ		◉	
1.0	-	10	▲		◒							◉	
3.8	60	-	▲									◉	
5.5	250	-	▲		◒								
			▲										
8.0	250	-	▲		◒								
13.8	790	70	▲			✳							
19.0	-	880	▲		◒		🍴	⊕		ℹ		◉	
5.0	310	80										◉	
6.3	90	10	▲										
14.5	700	370	▲										
3.6	-	220	▲										
			▲	○	◒		🍴					◉	
10.9	490	510	▲										🚡
15.4	-	750		○			🍴	⊕				◉	🚡

Stage	Place	Altitude (m)	Walking time	Cum. stage time	Distance (km)
4	**Courmayeur**	**1226**	**20min**	**5hr 30min**	**1.1**
5	Rifugio Bertone	1989	2hr	2hr	4.3
5	**Rifugio Bonatti**	**2025**	**2hr 30min**	**4hr 30min**	**7.7**
6	*Lavachey*	*1700*	*+45min*		
6	Arnouva	1784	1hr 40min	1hr 40min	5.5
6	Rifugio Elena	2062	50min	2hr 30min	2.4
6	La Peule	2071	2hr 20min	4hr 50min	6.0
6	Ferret	1705	1hr	5hr 50min	3.9
6	*Gîte de la Léchère*	*1700*	*+10min*		
6	**La Fouly**	**1610**	**40min**	**6hr 30min**	**2.7**
7	Praz-de-Fort/Arlache	1151	2hr 15min	2hr 15min	8.3
7	Issert	1055	30min	2hr 45min	2.0
7	**Champex**	**1467**	**1hr 45min**	**4hr 30min**	**4.7**
8	Champex d'en Haut	1444	40min	40min	2.5
8	Plan de l'Au	1330	30min	1hr 10min	2.2
8	Bovine	1987	2hr	3hr 10min	4.7
8	Col de la Forclaz	1526	1hr 40min	4hr 50min	4.5
8	**Trient**	**1279**	**40min**	**5hr 30min**	**2.1**
9	Le Peuty	1328	15min	15min	1.2
9	Col de Balme	2191	2hr 20min	2hr 35min	4.8
9	*Charamillon*	*1900*	*+35min*		
9	*Le Tour*	*1460*	*+1hr 5min*		
9	**Tré-le-Champ**	**1417**	**2hr 55min**	**5hr 30min**	**8.0**

Cum. stage distance (km)	Ascent (m)	Descent (m)	▲	○	◈	🍴	🍺	€	ⓘ	▣	▣	🚠
16.5	**40**	**20**	▲	○		🍴	🍺	€	ⓘ		▣	🚠
4.3	760	-	▲									
12.0	**330**	**290**	▲									
				○							▣	
5.5	150	390		○		🍴					▣	
7.9	290	10	▲									
13.9	490	480	▲									
17.8	20	380		○							▣	
			▲									
20.5	**20**	**120**	▲	○	◈	🍴	🍺	€	ⓘ		▣	
8.3	70	530	▲			🍴					▣	
10.3	10	100				🍴					▣	
15.0	**450**	**40**	▲	○	◈	🍴	🍺	€	ⓘ		▣	
2.5	30	60	▲									
4.7	30	140				🍴						
9.4	680	20				🍴						
13.9	150	610		○	◈	🍴	🍺				▣	
16.0	**-**	**250**	▲			🍴	🍺				▣	
1.2	50	-	▲		◈							
6.0	810	-	▲									🚠
			▲			🍴						🚠
			▲			🍴					▣	🚠
14.0	**240**	**1010**	▲		✱					▣	▣	

Stage	Place	Altitude (m)	Walking time	Cum. stage time	Distance (km)
10	*Gîte le Moulin*	*1350*	*+15min*		
10	*Lac Blanc*	*2352*	*+3hr*		
10	**La Flégère**	**1875**	**3hr 30min**	**3hr 30min**	**7.0**
11	junction above Planpraz	2080	2hr 15min	2hr 15min	5.1
11	Le Brévent	2525	1hr 30min	3hr 45min	2.8
11	Bellachat	2152	45min	4hr 30min	2.6
11	**Les Houches**	**1007**	**2hr 30min**	**7hr**	**7.5**
Alternative stages					
1A	**Les Houches**	**1007**	-	-	-
1A	Col de Voza	1657	2hr 30min	2hr 30min	6.0
1A	*Hotel Le Prarion*	*1860*	*+30min*		
1A	Bellevue	1801	+20min	2hr 50min	1.0
1A	Chalets de Miage	1550	3hr	5hr 50min	6.8
1A	Le Truc	1717	40min	6hr 30min	1.6
1A	**Les Contamines**	**1161**	**1hr 15min**	**7hr 45min**	**3.6**
1A	*Le Pontet*	*1180*	*+40min*		
8A	**Champex**	**1467**	-	-	-
8A	Arpette	1627	45min	45min	2.4
8A	Chalet du Glacier	1577	5hr 15min	6hr	9.1
8A	*Refuge Le Peuty*	*1328*	*+30min*		
8A	*Col de la Forclaz*	*1526*	*+45min*		
8A	*Refuge les Grands*	*2113*	*+1hr 30min*		
8A	**Trient**	**1279**	**1hr**	**7hr**	**4.0**

Cum. stage distance (km)	Ascent (m)	Descent (m)	Facilities									
			▲									
			▲		*							
7.0	**800**	**340**	▲		*	🍴						🚠
5.1	340	140				🍴						🚠
7.9	490	40				🍴						🚠
10.5	20	390	▲									
18.0	**40**	**1190**	▲	○	◬	🍴	⊕	⊞	ⓘ	⊙	⊙	🚠
–	–	–	▲	○	◬	🍴	⊕	⊞	ⓘ	⊙	⊙	🚠
6.0	660	20				🍴				⊙		
				○	*							
7.0	140	–				🍴				⊙		🚠
13.8	470	700	▲		*							
15.4	180	20	▲		*							
19.0	–	**560**	▲	○		🍴	⊕	⊞	ⓘ	⊙		
			▲		◬					⊙		
–	–	–	▲	○	◬	🍴	⊕	⊞	ⓘ	⊙		
2.4	170	10	▲		◬							
11.5	1060	1110				🍴						
			▲		◬							
				○	◬	🍴	⊕			⊙		
			▲									
15.5	–	**300**	▲			🍴	⊕			⊙		

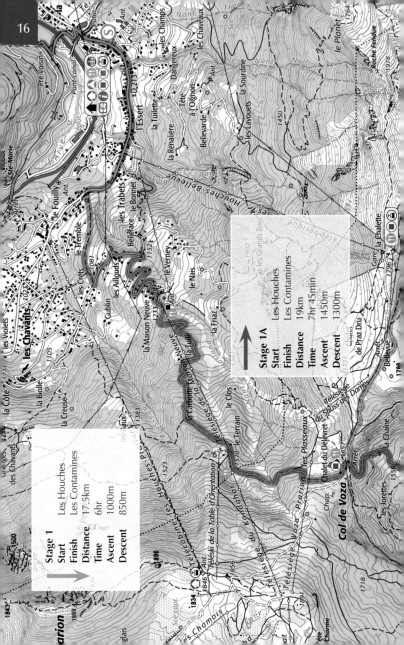

Stage 1

Start	Les Houches
Finish	Les Contamines
Distance	17.5km
Time	6hr
Ascent	1000m
Descent	850m

Stage 1A

Start	Les Houches
Finish	Les Contamines
Distance	19km
Time	7hr 45min
Ascent	1450m
Descent	1300m

Gla

Mont Lachat 2115
Col du Mont Lachat

Arrêt

2069

le Nid d'Aigle
2372

2390

Echelle

le Nid d'Aigle

2204

2153

l'Are

les Vrets

l'Are

Echelle

Pile

1732

Chalets de Tricot

2663

Combe des Juments

Passage des Recorbes

Chalet du Chalère

le Planet

1562

la Chapiot

Sur les Maures

Pont des Places

1413

Combe de Tricot

Col de Tricot

2120

Deux Frères

1966

N219

2132

la Maisonnette

le Crozat

la Pierre

Scécapt.

1891

Sur le Cart

les Bettières

la Fontaine

1743

Chalet de Presbert

1749

Chalet de Presbert

Map continues on page 18–19

1143

la Joux

Grand Plan

le Tranchet

1405

1526

Bionnassay

Pile

Chap.

l'Ormey

1298

1068

la Côte

Pile

le Champel

Chap.

1300

1205

la Villette

1045

les Chosalets

le Bon Nant

1080

les Maisons

les Thovex

1580

Chalet des Theux

le Mont

1316

Bionnassay

Joux

Plan

chet

Map continues on page 18–19

Stage 1 (CLOCKWISE)

Start	Les Contamines
Finish	Les Houches
Distance	17.5km
Time	5hr 45min
Ascent	850m
Descent	1000m

Stage 1A (CLOCKWISE)

Start	Les Contamines
Finish	Les Houches
Distance	19km
Time	7hr 15min
Ascent	1300m
Descent	1450m

Stage 2

Start	Les Contamines
Finish	Les Chapieux
Distance	19km
Time	7hr 30min
Ascent	1350m
Descent	960m

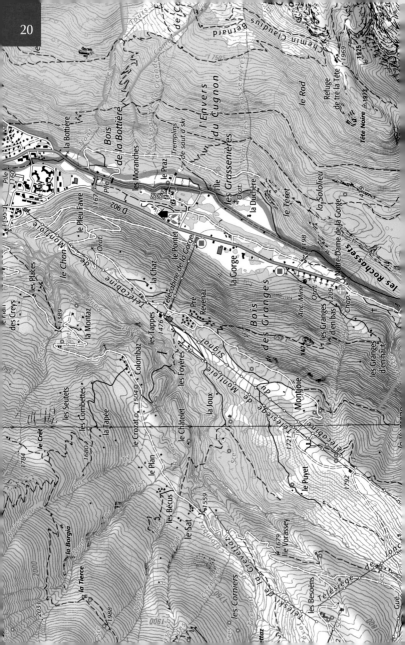

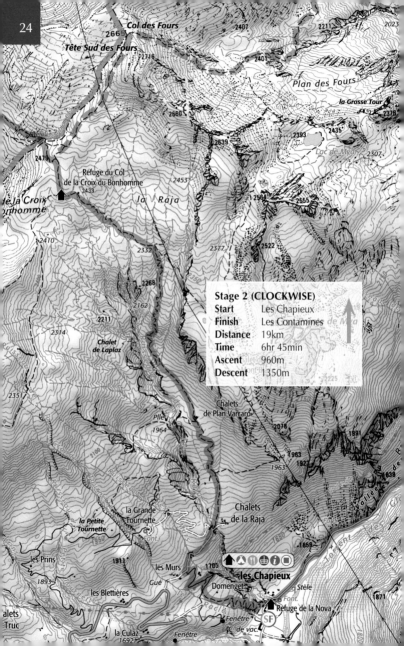

Col des Fours
2665
Tête Sud des Fours
2716

Plan des Fours
2407
2401
2023
2211

la Grosse Tour
2660
2376
2639
2393
2435
Lac de Myor
2307

2479
Refuge du Col
de la Croix du Bonhomme
2433
2453
la Raja
2564
2655

de la Croix
Bonhomme
2410
2377
2522
2377
2332

2268
2162
2211
2314
Chalet
de Laplaz

2351

Stage 2 (CLOCKWISE)
Start Les Chapieux
Finish Les Contamines
Distance 19km
Time 6hr 45min
Ascent 960m
Descent 1350m

Chalets
de Plan Varraro
2078
1891

Pllez
1964
1963
1923
1963
638

la Grande
Tournette
la Petite
Tournette
les Prins
1911
Chalets
de la Raja

1859
1893
les Murs
1705
Gué
les Blettières
les Chapieux
Stèle
871

alets
Truc
la Culaz
1692
Fenêtre
C. de vac.
Domenget
SF Refuge de la Nova
Fenêtre

Stage 3

Start	Les Chapieux
Finish	Rifugio Elisabetta
Distance	14.5km
Time	5hr
Ascent	1100m
Descent	460m

Combe Noire

2582

2514

2511

2448

2957

2812

les Cabottes

2389

2307

e Ecaille

de la Tépiaz

Val des Glaciers

le Bouillu
des Lanchettes
Plle

1998

Bnes f

2173

1932

les Marmottières

2294

2375

2478

2161

Tête
es Lanchons

2260

1975

1957

Chalets des Lanchettes

Sce

Sces

Ruisseau

2236

2142

la

23

Lanchier oulquière

Chalets
de Bellaval

2108

1973

le Gollier

Chalet-Refuge
des Mottets

Stèle

2305

le Bouillu
des Mottets

1868

SF

1846

le Rocher

Plle

les Mottets

2193

Ruisseau

2208

Grand

Maison Longe

le Clapey

la Ville
des Glaciers

Mon.

Ruisseau de la C

1781

1789

Chap

2072

2498

Chail

Mon

2695

2727

2722

les Pyramides Calcaires
2422
2496
Igne des Glaciers
2280
Alpe sup.
de la Lée Blanche
Rnes
2286
Vallon de la Lée B
2290
2400
res
Col de la Seigne
2603
Col d
front. 0.6
Orient
irn front. 2516
Bne front. 1.1
Mont Léchaud
2805
2602
Collet
de la Seigne
2894
2629
2591
e
i
g
n
e
2625
34
Glacier de Ch
Pointe Léchaud
28
Bassa Serra
2900
2836
Passage de Léchaud
2886
293
Glacier du
2875
2630
2841
3075
Pointe des Ouillons
3110
2638

Mt Blanc

3424

3200

2958

2134

3257

Biv. du Petit Mont Blanc
ou Rainetto
3047

2138

2985

M t Suc

2138

2839

Aig
de Combal

2138

2830

2708

1958

2807

Stage 3 (CLOCKWISE)
Start	Rifugio Elisabetta
Finish	Les Chapieux
Distance	14.5km
Time	4hr 15min
Ascent	460m
Descent	1100m

2180

Lac de Combal

2063

1970

2035

(SF)

Rif. Elisabetta Soldini

Alpe inf.
de la Lée Blanche

Aries
Orot.

Stage 4
Start	Rifugio Elisabetta
Finish	Courmayeur
Distance	16.5km
Time	5hr 30min
Ascent	530m
Descent	1500m

Lée Blanche

2280

Jardin du Miage

Le Jardin
du Miage

1762

1867

1935

1958

Chalet du
Miage

2012

1770

Miage

l'Arp Vieille inf.
2073   Rnes

V

V

A

L

2297

l'Arp Vieille sup.
2303

Mont Fortin

Mont Favre
2967

2811

2616

2867

Pré Pascal
1903

Peindein

Teleski

2 000

la Saxe

1226

Mont Chétif 2343 Mon. à la Madone

Courba Dzeleuna

Télésiège
Dzeleuna

Entrelevie

Larzey

1223

la Villette

1897

Télésiège de Dzeleuna

Plan Chécrouit

Télécabine

Dolonne

Téléphérique de Courmayeur

Dolonne

Maison Vieille

1697

Rvoir   Teleski

la Goletta

Torrent de Dolonne

1 700

1213

Tunnel

la Vittoria

Doire Baltée

SF

Viaduc

A 5

S 26d

Grange Praleni   1648

Champtorel

**Val Veny variant
continued from above**

1310   1306

Chap.   Tunnel

Entrèves

109

N.D.
de la Guerison

S 26d   A 5

Plan Ponquier

1505

Val Veny   1297

1289   Pa

12

Téléphérique

Pré Pascal
1903

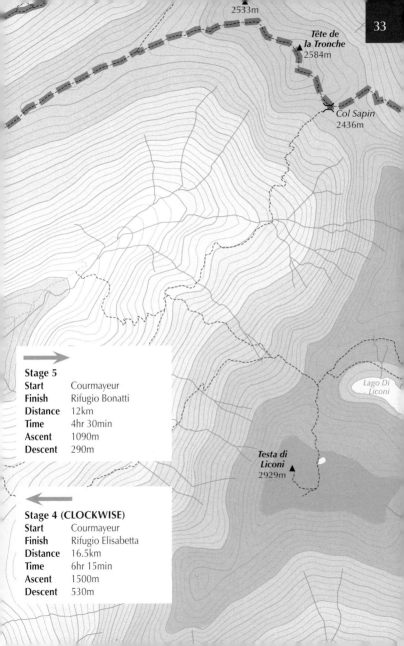

2533m

**Tête de
la Tronche**
2584m

Col Sapin
2436m

*Lago Di
Liconi*

**Testa di
Liconi**
2929m

Stage 5	
Start	Courmayeur
Finish	Rifugio Bonatti
Distance	12km
Time	4hr 30min
Ascent	1090m
Descent	290m

Stage 4 (CLOCKWISE)	
Start	Courmayeur
Finish	Rifugio Elisabetta
Distance	16.5km
Time	6hr 15min
Ascent	1500m
Descent	530m

2607

2580

1960

2173

2145

sup.
1653
du Milieu

Pra Sec

Pile
inf

1887

Tronchey

1620

1618 de Golf

le Pont

Chap

1616

Ferret   Terrain

L

Meyenzet

1902

la Leche

2115

A

Chap.

1627

Neyrun

2041

V

cieux

1889

1954

la

Daire

G...

2300

1564

Testa
Bernar
▲
2533

Leuchey

1923

Mont de la Saxe

2032

2115

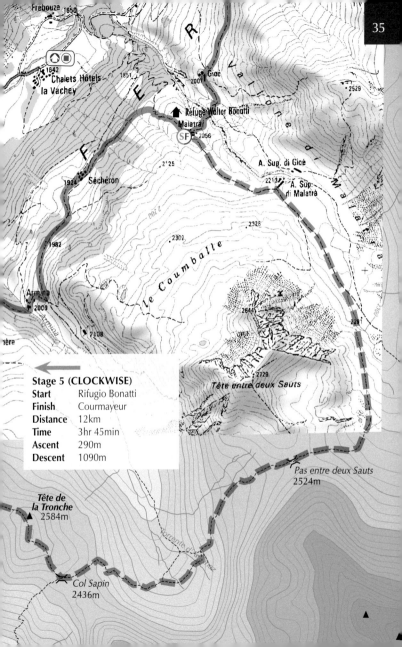

Frebouze 1650

Chalets Hôtels
la Vachey
1642

Giọé
2007

1851

2529

Réfuge Walter Bonatti
Malatrài
SF 2056

A. Sug. di Gioé

2125

A. Sùp.
di Malatrà
2213

Sécheron
1924

2200

2328

2308

le Coumballe

1982

2646

Armina
2009

7108

2221

ière

2729

Tête entre deux Sauts

Stage 5 (CLOCKWISE)

Start	Rifugio Bonatti
Finish	Courmayeur
Distance	12km
Time	3hr 45min
Ascent	290m
Descent	1090m

Pas entre deux Sauts
2524m

Tête de
la Tronche
2584m

torrente d...

Col Sapin
2436m

Bella Comba
▲
2701m

Stage 6	
Start	Rifugio Bonatti
Finish	La Fouly
Distance	20.5km
Time	6hr 30min
Ascent	970m
Descent	1380m

Ferrache

Rifuge Walter Bonatti

Malatrà

Vallone di Mal

Stage 7

Distance	La Fouly
Distance	Champex
Distance	15km
Time	4hr 30min
Ascent	530m
Descent	670m

Stage 6 (CLOCKWISE)

Distance	La Fouly
Distance	Rifugio Bonatti
Distance	20.5km
Time	7hr 15min
Ascent	1380m
Descent	970m

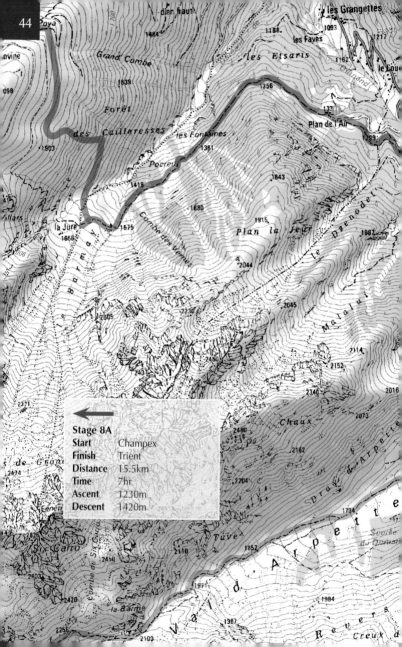

Stage 8A

Start	Champex
Finish	Trient
Distance	15.5km
Time	7hr
Ascent	1230m
Descent	1420m

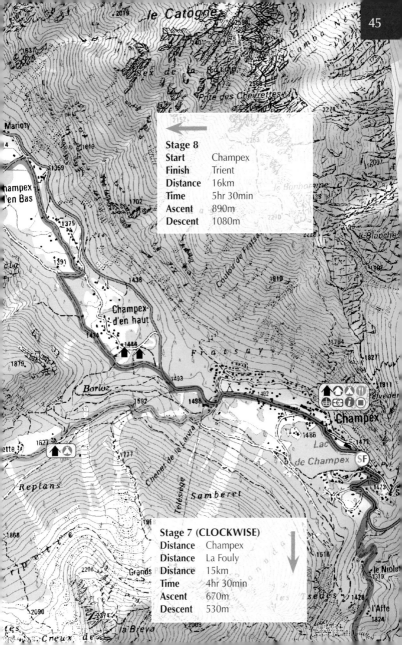

Stage 8
Start Champex
Finish Trient
Distance 16km
Time 5hr 30min
Ascent 890m
Descent 1080m

Stage 7 (CLOCKWISE)
Distance Champex
Distance La Fouly
Distance 15km
Time 4hr 30min
Ascent 670m
Descent 530m

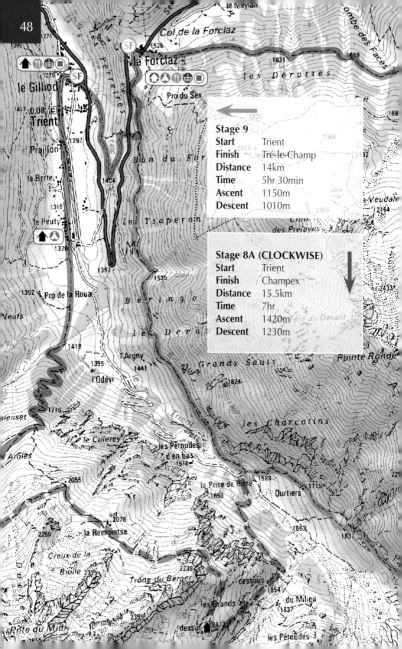

Stage 9

Start	Trient
Finish	Tré-le-Champ
Distance	14km
Time	5hr 30min
Ascent	1150m
Descent	1010m

Stage 8A (CLOCKWISE)

Start	Trient
Finish	Champex
Distance	15.5km
Time	7hr
Ascent	1420m
Descent	1230m

49

Stage 8 (CLOCKWISE)

Start	Trient
Finish	Champex
Distance	16km
Time	5hr 30min
Ascent	1080m
Descent	890m

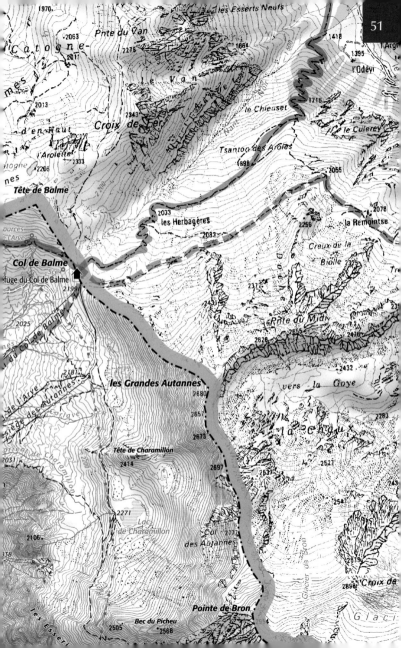

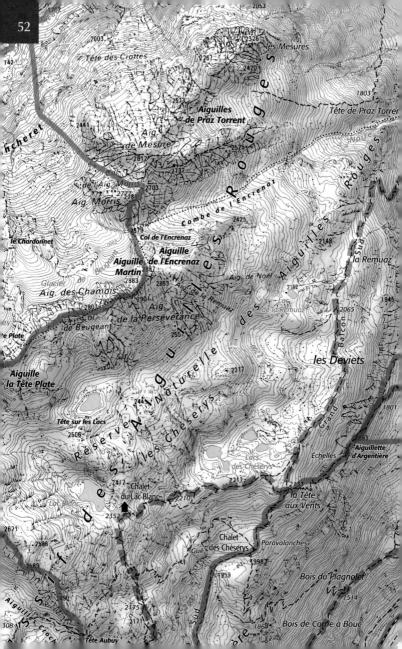

les Mesures

Tête des Crottes

Aiguilles de Praz Torrent

Tête de Praz Torrer

Aig. de Mesure

Combe de l'Encrenaz

le Chardonnet

Col de l'Encrenaz

Aig Morris

Aiguille de l'Encrenaz

Aiguille Martin

la Remuaz

Aig des Aiguilles

Aig de Noël

Lac de la Remuaz

Glacier de Aig. des Chamois

Aig de la Perseverance

Col de Beugeant

Plate

les Deviets

Réserve Naturelle des Cheserys

Aiguille la Tête Plate

Tête sur les Lacs

Lac Blanc

Aiguillette d'Argentière

Échelles

Lacs des Chéserys

Chalet du Lac Blanc

la Tête aux Vents

Chalet des Chéserys

Gué

Paravalanches

Bois du Plagnolet

Bois de Corne à Bouc

Tête Aubuy

Aiguilles Croix

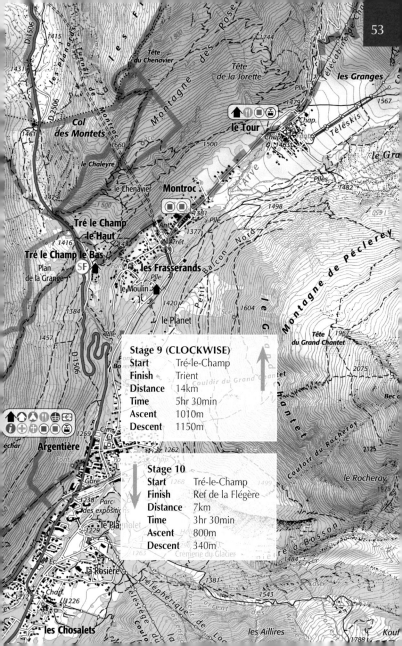

Stage 9 (CLOCKWISE)

Start	Tré-le-Champ
Finish	Trient
Distance	14km
Time	5hr 30min
Ascent	1010m
Descent	1150m

Stage 10

Start	Tré-le-Champ
Finish	Ref de la Flégère
Distance	7km
Time	3hr 30min
Ascent	800m
Descent	340m

Stage 10 (CLOCKWISE)

Start	Ref de la Flégère
Finish	Tré-le-Champ
Distance	7km
Time	3hr 15min
Ascent	340m
Descent	800m

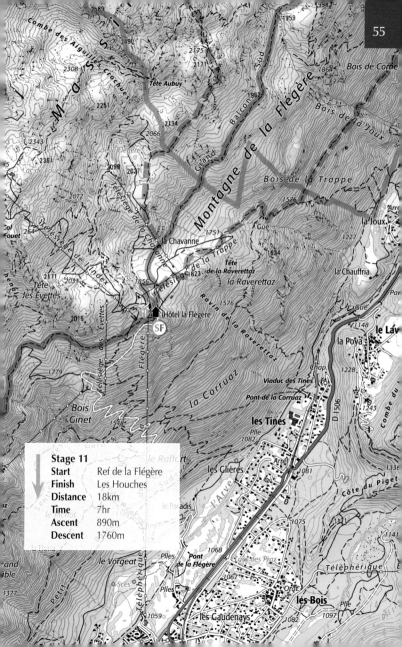

Stage 11
Start   Ref de la Flégère
Finish   Les Houches
Distance   18km
Time   7hr
Ascent   890m
Descent   1760m

Barrage
de la Bajulaz

2225
Arête de Rochy
2079
1747
1525
Torrent
1743
1441
Combe de Rochy
1513
1450
1441
Diosa
1975
le Vieux Cheppy
1344
les Péchots
Monta
1168
Ravin des Bornes
la Larze
1807
le Grand Brie
2212
1659
1658
Ravin de la Larze
2024
1857
Ravin de Carlaveyron
2066
Creux du M
1935
2062
2159
2041
Chálets
de Carlaveyron
rve Naturelle de Carlaveyron
à Châtelet
Carlaveyron
5
2162
Tête
de Bellachat
la Vogealle
Frêtes de la Vogealle
2145
2142
2232
2117
Lac
des Aiguillette
2172
2241
2130
Aiguillette
des Houches
Col
de Bellachat
1987
2286
2308
2262
2241
Aiguillette
du Brévent
Pointe de Lapaz
2310
2313
Saléchet
Plan de Benoi
1922
Chalets
de Chailloux
1900
1782
les

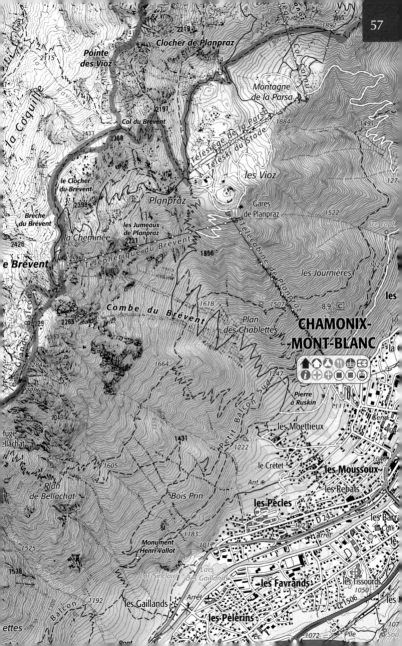

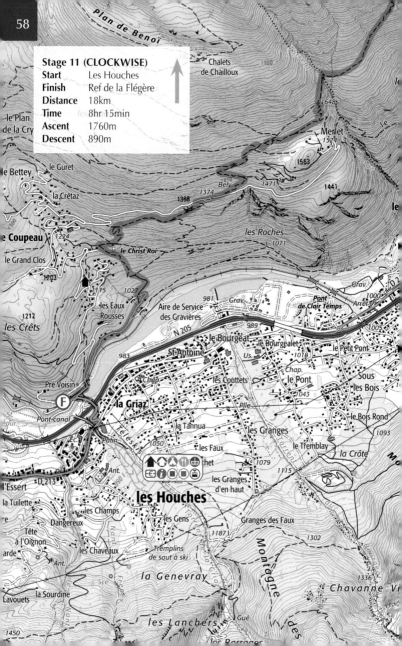

Stage 11 (CLOCKWISE)

Start	Les Houches
Finish	Ref de la Flégère
Distance	18km
Time	8hr 15min
Ascent	1760m
Descent	890m

TOWN MAPS

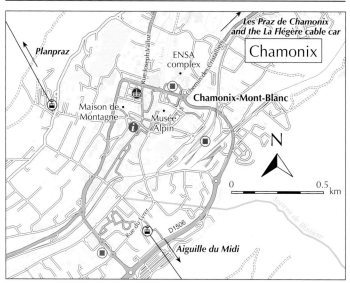

Les Praz de Chamonix and the La Flégère cable car

Planpraz

ENSA complex

Rue Joseph Vallot

Chemin des Cristalliers

Chamonix

Chamonix-Mont-Blanc

Maison de Montagne

Musée Alpin

N

0   0.5 km

Rue du Lyret

D1506

Torrent de Blaitière

Aiguille du Midi

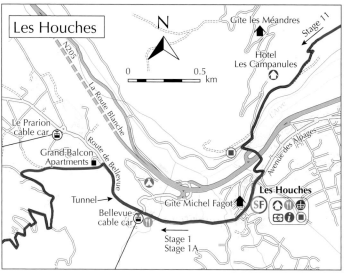

Les Houches

N205

La Route Blanche

N

0   0.5 km

Gîte les Méandres

Stage 11

Hotel Les Campanules

L'Arve

Le Prarion cable car

Route de Bellevue

Grand Balcon Apartments

Avenue des Alpages

Tunnel→

Gîte Michel Fagot

Les Houches

Bellevue cable car

Stage 1
Stage 1A

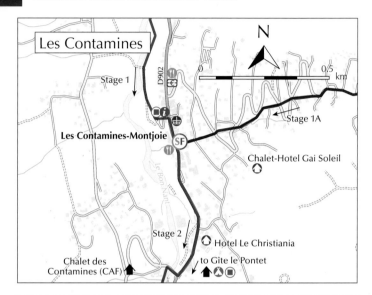

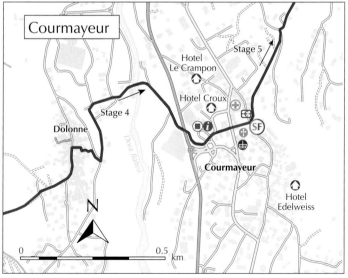

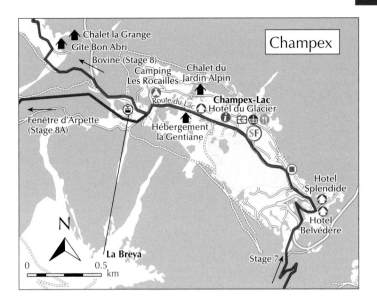

Champex

ACCOMMODATION LISTINGS

This list details accommodation in sequential order when following the anti-clockwise TMB route. The number of places and type of accommodation on offer, and dates

Stage	Name	Type	Facilities	Open
FRANCE				
1, 1A, 11	Camping Bellevue	⬤		June to September
1, 1A, 11	Gîte Michel Fagot	▲	28 dortoir places	all year
1, 1A, 11	Hotel Les Campanules	⬡	120 beds	end December to mid September
1, 1A, 11	Ibis Styles Les Houches Chamonix	⬡	44 rooms	all year
1, 1A	*Hotel Le Prarion*	⬡	*15 dortoir places, 14 beds*	*mid June to early September*
1	Chalet-Refuge du Fioux	▲	22 beds	May to September
1	Auberge de Bionnassay	▲	20 dortoir places, 18 beds	June to end September
1A	Refuge de Miage	▲	31 dortoir places, 4 rooms; camping permitted	June to mid September
1A	Auberge du Truc	▲	28 dortoir places, camping permitted	mid June to mid September
1, 1A	Chalet des Contamines	▲	20 dortoir places	mid June to mid September
1, 1A	Hotel Christiania	⬡	30 beds	
1, 1A	Chalet Hotel Gai Soleil	⬡	42 beds	
1, 1A	La Ferme à Piron	▲	12 beds	
1, 1A	Les Mélèzes	▲	12 beds	
1, 1A	Chalet Hotel La Chemenaz	⬡	40 rooms	
2	Gîte le Pontet	▲ ⬤	32 dortoir places, mini cabins and camping	June to late September
2	Refuge Nant Borrant	▲ ⬤	37 dortoir places	early June to late September
2	*Refuge des Prés*	▲	*30 dortoir places*	*mid June to end October*

when open, are given when known. Further details may be obtained from tourist offices. Additions or alterations would be welcomed by the authors. *NB*: international dialling codes for phone numbers are France 0033; Italy 0039; Switzerland 0041.

Tel	Web/email	Comments	Listed on montourdu montblanc .com
0633 503412	www.camping-bellevue-leshouches. com		
0450 544228	www.gite-fagot.com		Y
0450 544071	www.hotel-campanules.com		
0450 544009	https://all.accor.com	IBIS hotel	
0450 544007	www.prarion.com	*access from Les Houches/ Les Chavants via télécab- ine (gondola)*	
0450 934523			Y
0450 934523	www.auberge-bionnassay.com		Y
0450 969170	www.refugemiage.com		
0450 931248	aubergedutruc@hotmail.fr		Y
0450 470088			
0450 470272	www.lechristiania-hotel.com		
0450 470294	www.gaisoleil.com		
0745 084349	www.lafermeapiron.com		Y
0980 892218	bourdeu.eric@gmail.com		Y
0450 470244	www.chemenaz.com	south of Les Contamines	
0450 470404	www.campinglepontet.fr	south of Les Contamines	Y
0450 470357	refugenantborrant@free.fr	camping +10min from refuge	Y
0661 865043	*contact@lerefugedespres.com*	*+1hr 30min from Ref Nant Borrant*	Y

Stage	Name	Type	Facilities	Open
2	Refuge de la Balme	⬆ ◓	36 dortoir places, 4 beds	mid June to mid September
2	Refuge de la Croix du Bonhomme	⬆	105 dortoir places	mid June to mid September
2, 3	Refuge des Mottets	⬆	80 beds in dortoirs and rooms	mid June to mid September
2	Auberge de la Nova	⬆	30 dortoir places, 33 beds	May to early October
2	Chambres du Soleil	⬆	24 beds, small dortoirs and rooms	
2	Camping Les Chapieux	◓		open all year
3	*Refuge Robert Blanc*	⬆	*40 dortoir places*	
ITALY				
3	Rifugio Elisabetta	⬆	52 dortoir places, 24 beds	mid June to end September
4	Cabane du Combal	⬆	23 beds in 7 rooms	mid June to mid September
4	Rifugio Maison Vieille	⬆	35 dortoir places	mid June to end September
4	Rifugio le Randonneur	⬆	25 beds, 18 dortoir places and 2 rooms	late June to early September
4	*Rifugio Monte Bianco*	⬆	*70 places in dortoirs and beds*	*June to mid September*
4	*Camping Aiguille Noire*	◓	*on-site refreshments and shop*	
4	*Camping HOBO Val Veny Cuignon*	◓	*café, shop, tent rental (2 and 4 person)*	
4	*Camping la Sorgente*	◓	*pitches and camping pods/ chalets*	
4	Hotel Edelweiss	◓		
4	Hotel Crampon	◓		
4	Hotel Croux	◓		
4	Pensione Venezia	⬆		
5	Rifugio Giorgio Bertone	⬆	60 beds, mainly dortoir places, also rooms	mid June to mid September
5	Rifugio Bonatti	⬆	60 dortoir places	June to end September

Tel	Web/email	Comments	Listed on montourdu montblanc .com
0450 470354	www.refugedelabalme.com		Y
0479 070528	refugecroixdubonhomme.ffcam.fr		
0479 070170	refuge@lesmottets.com	Col des Fours variant (Stage 2); main route (Stage 3)	Y
0982 126435 (summer), 0664 949835 (off season)	www.refugelanova.com		Y
0479 313022	www.leschambresdusoleil-montblanc.com		Y
		free camping	
0479 072422	www.refugerobertblanc.fr	*off main route at 2760m*	
0165 844080	www.rifugioelisabetta.com		
0165 1756421	cabaneducombal@gmail.com		Y
337 230979	www.maisonvieille.com		Y
349 536 8898	www.randonneurmb.com		Y
0165 869097	www.rifugiomontebianco.eu	*via Rifugio Maison Vieille or Val Veny variants*	Y
0351 804 8846	www.aiguillenoire.com	*Val Veny variant*	
0165 869073	*info@campinghobo.com*	*Val Veny variant*	
0389 902 0772	*info@campinglasorgente.net*	*via Val Veny variant (off route)*	
0165 841590	info@albergoedelweiss.it		
0165 842385	www.crampon.it		
0165 846735	www.hotelcroux.it		
0165 842461	pensionevenezia@gmail.com		
347 032 5785	www.rifugiobertone.it		Y
0165 1827229; mob 0335 6848 578	www.rifugiobonatti.it		

Stage	Name	Type	Facilities	Open
5	Hotel Lavachey	⊖	21 beds	mid June to mid September
6	Chalet Val Ferret	⊖	21 beds in 7 rooms	June to mid September
6	Rifugio Elena	▲	127 beds in dortoirs and rooms for 2–4 people	mid June to mid September
SWITZERLAND				
6	Alpage de la Peule	▲	33 places in dortoirs	mid June to mid September
6	Hotel du Col de Fenêtre	⊖	37 beds, 18 dortoir places, 7 rooms with 2–4 beds	mid June to mid September
6	Gîte de la Léchère	▲	27 dortoir places	June to late September
6	Chalet Le Dolent	▲	30 beds in dortoirs and rooms	all year
6	Auberge des Glaciers	▲	56 beds: 42 in small dortoirs and 7 rooms	open all year
6	Hotel Edelweiss	⊖	60 beds, 20 dortoir places, 20 rooms	mid June to late September
6	Refuge Maya-Joie	▲	45 beds in dortoirs and rooms	May to end September
6	Gîte de la Fouly	▲	17 beds in rooms and dortoir	
6	Camping des Glaciers	⊛		
7	Chambre d'hôte Croquenature	⊖	7 beds in 3 rooms	
7	Hotel Splendide	⊖		
7	Hotel Bélvèdere	⊖		
7	Chalet du Jardin Alpin	▲	12 dortoir places, 2 rooms, self-catering only	May to end October
7	Hotel du Glacier	⊖	double and triple rooms	
7	Hébergement la Gentiane	▲		
7	Pension en Plan Air	▲	62 dortoir places	
7	Camping Les Rocailles	⊛		open all year

Tel	Web/email	Comments	Listed on montourdu montblanc .com
0165 869723	www.lavachey.com		Y
0165 844959	www.chaletvalferret.com		Y
0165 844688	info@rifugioelena.it		
027 783 1041 (summer), 079 290 3493 (off season)	nicolas.lapeule@gmail.com		Y
027 783 1188; mob 079 134 96 70	hotelducoldefenetre@gmail.com		Y
027 783 3064 (summer); mob 079 862 98 37	www.lalechere.ch		Y
027 783 2931	www.dolent.ch		Y
027 7831171	www.aubergedesglaciers.ch		Y
027 783 2621	www.fouly.ch		Y
027 565 5630	www.mayajoie.ch		Y
027 565 0653	www.gitedelafouly.ch		Y
027 783 1826	https://camping-glaciers.ch	chalets, caravans and tents to rent	
079 509 1424	www.croquenature.ch	in Arlaches, 5 min north of Praz-de-Fort	
027 783 1145	www.hotel-splendide.ch		
027 783 1114	www.le-belvedere.ch		
027 783 1217	reservation@flore-alpe.ch	only bookable for 2 nights or more	
027 782 6151	www.hotelglacier.ch		
079 195 8381		rooms above patisserie	
027 783 2350	pensionenpleinair@gmail.com	best for groups	
027 783 1979	www.champex-camping.ch	substantial site at the top end of the village	

Stage	Name	Type	Facilities	Open
8	Gîte Bon Abri	▲	50 dortoir places, 2 double rooms	June to end September
8	Chalet La Grange	▲	12 beds in rooms and small dortoir	mid June to mid September
8A	Relais d'Arpette	▲ ◒	120 beds, 86 dortoir places, rooms, pods, camping	May to mid October
8, 8A	Hotel du Col de la Forclaz	◒	65 beds, 38 dortoir places and rooms	mid December to November
8, 8A	Camping de l'Arpille	◒		
8	Auberge du Mont Blanc	▲	120 beds, 60 dortoir places, 20 rooms	June to end September
8	La Grande Ourse	▲	80 beds, 38 dortoir places, 18 rooms plus apartments	mid June to late September
8, 8A, 9	Refuge Le Peuty	▲ ◒	19 dortoir places, yurt for 2–4 people	June to end September
8, 8A, 9	Refuge Les Grands	▲	15 dortoir places	mid June to mid October
FRANCE				
9	Refuge du Col de Balme	▲	26 dortoir places	mid June to mid September
9	Chalet de Balme	▲	22 dortoir places, 2 geopods	open all year
9	Gîte d'Alpage Les Ecuries de Charamillon	▲	19 beds	mid June to mid September
9	Chalet Alpin du Tour (FFCAM)	▲	86 places	April to mid September
9	Auberge la Boërne	▲	31 dortoir places plus camping	open all year
9	Le Moulin	▲	38 dortoir places	mid December to end September
10	Refuge du Lac Blanc	▲	40 dortoir places	manned from mid June to end September
10	Refuge de la Flégère	▲	66 dortoir places, 21 beds	mid June to mid September
11	Refuge Bellachat	▲	24 dortoir places	late June to mid September
11	Gîte Les Méandres	▲	24 beds	during the walking season

Tel	Web/email	Comments	Listed on montourdu montblanc.com
027 783 1423	www.gite-bonabri.com		Y
079 948 7576	www.lagrangechampex.com		Y
027 783 1221	www.arpette.ch		Y
027 722 2688		main route Stage 8; variant route Stage 8A	Y
027 722 2688	colforclazhotel@bluewin.ch	next to Hotel du Col de la Forclaz	
077 420 0814	www.aubergemontblanc.com		Y
079 591 5091, 027 722 1754	www.la-grande-ourse.ch		Y
078 719 2983	info@refugelepeuty.ch	camping in field opposite	Y
026 660 6504	self-catering accommodation only: cooking facilities, water supply, infrequently wardened	main route Stage 8; variant routes Stage 8A and 9	
0607 061630	www.refugeducoldebalme.com	use +33 (French phone prefix)	
0666 194988	www.chalet-de-balme.fr	below Col des Posettes	
0450 541707; mob 0670 128504	www.les-ecuries-de-charamillon.fr	*via Le Tour variant*	Y
0450 540416	chaletdutour.ffcam.fr	*via Le Tour variant*	
0450 540514	www.la-boerne.fr		Y
0682 333454	www.gite-chamonix.com	in Les Frasserands, south of Tré-le-Champ	Y
0767 567414	www.refuge-lac-blanc.fr	*via high-level variant*	
0603 582814	www.refuge-de-la-flegere.com		
0789 033038	www.refuge-bellachat.com		
0450 545666	www.tupilak.com		Y

CAMPING ON THE TMB

Official campsites and emplacements

Official campsites and/or *emplacements* are located in the following places, listed sequentially on an anti-clockwise TMB. They are marked on maps and facilities listings with a ⛺ camping symbol.

Les Houches (near the Bellevue cableway) – Stage 1, 1A

Les Contamines (+40min at Le Pontet) – Stage 1, 1A

Emplacements after **Ref Nant Borrant** and near **Ref de la Balme** – Stage 2

Les Chapieux – Stage 2

Val Veny (below Rif Monte Bianco, via variant route) – Stage 4

Italian Val Ferret (off route) – Stage 5

La Fouly (below the village) – Stage 6

Champex-Lac (upper end) – Stage 7

Relais d'Arpette (for Fenêtre d'Arpette route) – Stage 8A

Col de la Forclaz – Stage 8, 8A

Le Peuty – Stage 8, 8A, 9

Argentière (off route) – Stage 9

Bivouac camping

The following refuges may allow overnight bivouac camping (small tents pitched between sunset and sunrise only). Always ask permission at the refuge; a small payment is sometimes required. Bivouac camping is not allowed in Italy or Switzerland. They are not marked with a campsite symbol on the maps, but are indicated in the Stage Facilities Planner with an ✳ asterisk.

Chalet-Hotel le Prarion (+30min from Col de Voza) – Stage 1, 1A

Refuge du Fioux – Stage 1

Refuge de Miage – Stage 1A

Auberge du Truc – Stage 1A

Refuge de la Croix du Bonhomme – Stage 2

Gîte Bon Abri (only if Camping Les Rocailles in Champex-Lac is full) – Stage 8, 8A

Auberge la Boërne – Stage 9

Refuge du Lac Blanc – Stage 10 (very limited space)

Refuge de la Flégère – Stage 10

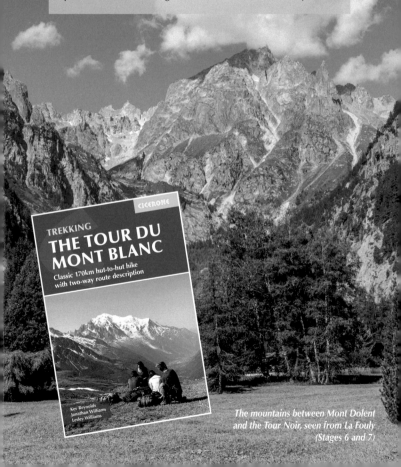

CICERONE

TREKKING
THE TOUR DU MONT BLANC
Classic 170km hut-to-hut hike with two-way route description

Kev Reynolds
Jonathan Williams
Lesley Williams

The mountains between Mont Dolent and the Tour Noir, seen from La Fouly (Stages 6 and 7)